Park Bench Memories

Haiku Tailwinds

~~~

Gary Hotham

Yiqralo Press
2020
~~~

Park Bench Memories: Haiku Tailwinds

Yiqralo Press
Scaggsville, Maryland, USA

Photos by the author:

Cover: Bench on York Beach, Maine, October 2012
Tall Thin Tree: Hersey, Pennsylvania, April 2012
Book, Hands and Glass Tumblers: BWI Airport, April 2012
Selfie in Man Cave: Scaggsville, Maryland, July 2020
No Feet Shadow: Scaggsville, Maryland, July 2018,
Back Cover: Swamp on Thompkins Road,
Presque Isle, Maine, September 2018

And thanks to Michael Dylan Welch
for helpful format advice.

Remembering

Hilma Weinsheimer Haiges
1915–1991

daughter, sister, wife, daughter-in-law,
mother, aunt, mother-in-law,
grandmother,
child of God

all those nouns sat well with her

holding up the snowfall
the park bench
in her memory

rattling back
a near empty bottle
of vitamins

by phone
too far away to hear the snow
in the goodbye

hospice walls
a print of the famous
still life

story time
our grandson finds words
not written down

city limits
the wind losing
touch

his death snuck by me
last night's storm measured
in the rain gauge

crossing paths
yesterday's fallen leaves
with today's

no names
to wear away
the unknowns at Gettysburg

each afternoon
too many crickets to hear
one more

gray winter light
the only breath we hear
my brother's last

far from home
sunlight has its own place
on the floor

sunrise at Gettysburg
between unknowns
a full name as silent

over the giveaway table
clouds that don't need
a wind

The Louvre
one of the faces in the crowd
Mona Lisa

bringing up memories
fog hiding
itself

one country to the next
rain covered
road

shaking the snow globe
each time the same sound
of falling

close
to the odor
rocks the ocean keeps smooth

shaping
imaginations
summer clouds

hiding
all of mine
mountain silence

in the night
the phone number
my parents had

sea fog
a way to hear
the rocks

passing shower
words the rain takes
from us

sunrise coffee
one mountainside
at a time

shade for the longest day of the year

—

clouds we'll never feel again

sleeping dog
the storm runs out of
snow

night crawls in
our grandson knows how fast
to read a picture book

after the burial
her clothes hanging
by themselves

light stutters
sunrise

Personal Versus Impersonal

"[W]e learn something very important about the biblical worldview. In Scripture, the personal is greater than the impersonal. The impersonal things and forces in this world are created and directed by a personal God. . . . Matter, energy, motion, time, and space are under the rule of a personal Lord. All the wonderful things that we find in personality—intelligence, compassion, creativity, love, justice—are not ephemeral data, doomed to be snuffed out in cosmic calamity; rather, they are aspects of what is most permanent, most ultimate. They are what the universe is really all about."

John M. Frame, *The Doctrine of God*,
P&R Publishing, 2002, page 26

Some years ago, during a talk with college students, I suggested they find a good systematic theologian to read and study. Whether you agree or not with all that theologian wrote, reading such a thinker broadens and deepens one's understanding of God because the systematic theologian deals with topics most of us do not have the time, energy or ability for. Many years ago, I discovered John Frame, a systematic theologian who writes with clarity and insight. His point about personal versus impersonal is a valuable and important foundation for the work of a poet. There is nothing more personal than a poem or haiku.

"It is he who made the earth by his power, who established the world by his wisdom, and by his understanding stretched out the heavens. When he utters his voice there is a tumult of waters in the heavens, and he makes the mist rise from the ends of the earth. He makes lightning for the rain, and he brings forth the wind from his storehouses."

Jeremiah 51:15–16
English Standard Version

Acknowledgments

All the haiku have been previously published in the past ten years in the following publications:

Acorn
Akitsu Quarterly
Blithe Spirit
Frogpond
Haiku Canada Review
Sitting in the Sun: Haiku North America Anthology 2019
The Heron's Nest
Mariposa
Modern Haiku
Noon
Otata
Presence
Quadrant
Wales Haiku Journal
Upstate Dim Sum

Gary Hotham

Writing haiku since 1966

Appearing in journals, anthologies,
chapbooks and books

Making moments wear words